The Guide to Owning a **Cornish Rex Cat**

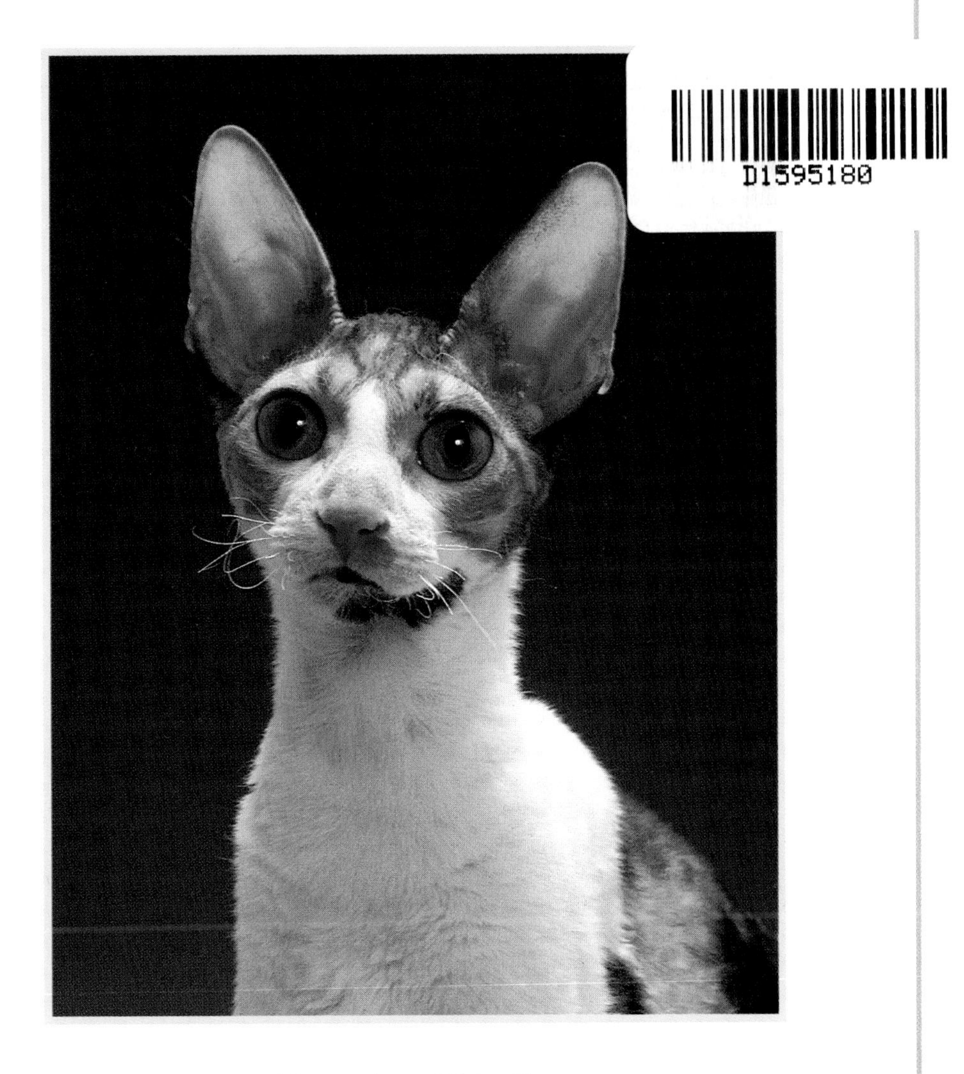

Greta Huls

CONTENTS

Dedication

For my family who always believed in me and for Cardell Vanessa of Rexphiles, who started my love affair with the Cornish Rex.

All photos by Isabelle Francais except the following: Michele Franklin (page 14), Diane Hammond (page 26), Greta Huls (pages 8, 19, 29, 35), Katja Kinnunen (page 5), R. G. Koehler-Jalbert (pages 12 [top], 13, 24), Julie Ledford (page 37), Art Nadelman (page 15), Wendy Nelson (page 59), Johnelle Odegard (page 9), Carol Page (pages 10, 18 [bottom], 57), Amy Pezzoni (pages 18 [top], 38), Heli Tepponen (page 28), Debbe Wiggs (page 22).

The publisher thanks the following owners of cats pictured in this book: Kathy G. Berke, Norma Berke, Cilka Castro, Jessica Everhart, Susan Ferguson, Michele and Georgette Franklin, Babette Gray, Diane Hammond, Greta Huls, Pat Huls, Bekke and Russell Jalbert, Christine W. Keightley, Katja Kinnunen and Heli Tepponen, Catherine A. Lachenmayer, Julie and Russell Ledford, Nancy Mindlin, Art and Emily Nadelman, Johnelle and Jessica Odegard, Carol Page, Amy Pezzoni, Judy Piesco, Theresa Rappa, Faith Sauvage, Eldon A. Smith, Charlene Smith, Paul and Dolores Spivack, Ellen S. Weiss, Debbe Wiggs.

RE 418

Distributed in the UNITED STATES to the Pet Trade by T.F.H. Publications, Inc., 1 TFH Plaza, Neptune City, NJ 07753; on the Internet at www.tfh.com; in CANADA by Rolf C. Hagen Inc., 3225 Sartelon St., Montreal, Quebec H4R 1E8; Pet Trade by H & L Pet Supplies Inc., 27 Kingston Crescent, Kitchener, Ontario N2B 2T6; in ENGLAND by T.F.H. Publications, PO Box 74, Havant PO9 5TT; in AUSTRALIA AND THE SOUTH PACIFIC by T.F.H. (Australia), Pty. Ltd., Box 149, Brookvale 2100 N.S.W., Australia; in NEW ZEALAND by Brooklands Aquarium Ltd., 5 McGiven Drive, New Plymouth, RD1 New Zealand; in SOUTH AFRICA by Rolf C. Hagen S.A. (PTY.) LTD., P.O. Box 201199, Durban North 4016, South Africa; in JAPAN by T.F.H. Publications. Published by T.F.H. Publications, Inc.

MANUFACTURED IN THE
UNITED STATES OF AMERICA
BY T.F.H. PUBLICATIONS, INC.

HISTORY OF THE CORNISH REX

Once upon a time, about 50 years ago, an unusual cat was born in Bodmin Moor, Cornwall, England. The golden moment was July 21, 1950. On that date, Serena, a normal tortoiseshell-and-white cat, gave birth to a litter of five kittens that included a strangely curly-coated, cream-colored male. In an earlier era, this magical cat might have been called a fairy changeling, because he had

The history of the Cornish Rex began in 1950 with one small curly-coated kitten (the ancestor of this little cutie), born to a normal-coated mother.

huge bat-like ears, a long tail, and a slender body. At first, the kitten's owner, Nina Ennismore, thought his coat would flatten when he dried, but instead the curls became more pronounced. She decided that he would make a good pet and took Kallibunker, as he was named, to her veterinarian to be neutered. However, the veterinarian recognized Kallibunker's genetic value and suggested that Ennismore contact geneticist A. C. Jude.

Jude agreed that Kallibunker was a genetic mutation and suggested that Kallibunker and Serena be mated together to strengthen the line. They were, and they had two curly kittens. Ennismore called this new breed "Rex," which came from her previous experience breeding curly-coated Rex rabbits. After a different Rex gene was discovered in 1960, the words "Cornish" and "Devon" were added by most fanciers to differentiate the two breeds.

It was discovered that the Cornish Rex mutation was a recessive gene, meaning that two Cornish Rex had to be bred together in order to have curly-coated kittens. Serena, Kallibunker's mother, obviously carried the gene that was necessary to provide the curly coat. Curly-coated cats had been reported for years in Cornwall, but Kallibunker was the first to be documented. When Kallibunker was bred to Siamese, Burmese, and British Shorthair cats, they would only have normal-coated kittens. However, these normal-coated kittens would carry the gene, so that when they were bred back to a Cornish Rex or each other, more curly-coated kittens were possible. These breedings changed the shape of Cornish Rex in Europe into a sturdier body type.

Kallibunker had had several offspring when Ennismore decided that the breeding program was too expensive. She tried to sell the cats but could not get a fair price, so unfortunately she had Kallibunker, who fought with another tom, and Serena euthanized. Kallibunker was survived by his sons, Sham Pain Charlie and Poldhu, and his granddaughter, La Morna Cove, all of which carried on the Cornish Rex breeding program.

CORNISH REX IN THE UNITED STATES

The Cornish Rex began to catch the eye of the American public and cat fanciers in 1956 after a story and photos of Kallibunker and one of his kittens appeared in *Life* magazine. La Morna Cove (also known as Lamorna Cove and La Morna in Great Britain) and her half-brother Pendennis Castle were imported in 1957 by Fran Blancheria of San Diego, California. Pendennis Castle, a red Cornish Rex, died before he sired any kittens, but La Morna, a blue, had been bred to her father, Poldhu, before leaving Great Britain. It is La Morna's kittens that established the Daz-

Zling and Fan-T-Cee lines, the foundation of the Cornish Rex in the US. La Morna and her kittens were bred to Siamese cats in an effort to widen the US gene pool, which resulted in the cats having a thinner, more Oriental body than Great Britain's cobbier Cornish Rex. Despite the early Siamese influence and pointed gene, the pointed Cornish Rex would not be accepted by the United States' Cat Fanciers' Association (CFA) for another 27 years.

European Cornish Rex like EC FIN*Darling-Isis' Earthling have a different body type than those in the United States.

CORNISH REX IN GREAT BRITAIN

Brian Stirling-Webb, a prominent British fancier and experimental breeder, purchased Poldhu from Ennismore in 1958. Poldhu was unusual, because he was an extremely rare fertile blue-cream male. However, when genetic tests were done to ensure his blue-cream status, the results left Poldhu sterile and the tissue sample was misplaced. It is certain, though, that Poldhu was a blue-cream because he sired red-and-cream female kittens with four different queens.

Once Poldhu became sterile, the only remaining fertile male Cornish Rex by 1960 was his brother, a cream-and-white called Sham Pain Charlie, also known in England as Champagne Chas.

A NEW REX MALE

There was great excitement in 1960 when a blue rex-coated male kitten named Kirlee was discovered by Beryl Cox in Buckfastleigh, Devon, England. His dam was a stray tortie-and-white, normal-coated cat that mated with a feral, curly-coated tom that lived in a nearby abandoned tin mine. It was hoped that Kirlee would be another fertile Rex male to help expand the critically limited gene pool. However, it was determined that the two genes were distinctly different after several breedings resulted in normal-coated kittens. Some of those kittens carried both rex genes, so many Cornish Rex show Devon Rex in their very early pedigrees.

Eventually, Alison Ashford of Great Britain imported Riovista Kismet, a blue Cornish Rex, from Jeanne Jeffrey of Calgary, Alberta, Canada. Kismet,

These Devon Rex cats are genetically different from Cornish Rex. Bred together, a Devon Rex and a Cornish Rex will produce kittens with straight coats.

Kallibunker's great-great-great-grandson, was brought to England to help the British Cornish Rex return to its original appearance. Ashford, who was deeply involved in the early breeding programs of both the Cornish and Devon Rex breeds, succeeded in breeding the first all-white Cornish Rex after four years of careful breeding. However, the English Cornish Rex continues to look heavier than the United States' Cornish Rex.

SHOW HISTORY IN THE UNITED STATES

To most of the world, the two Rex breeds immediately became known as the Cornish Rex and the Devon Rex. Only the CFA, the world's largest cat registry, continued to refuse to recognize the difference. The CFA began registering Rex cats in 1962, and the Rex breed was recognized by the CFA for championship status in 1964. Up until 1979, the Devon Rex had to be shown together with the Cornish Rex under the Rex name and with a standard written for the Cornish, causing a lot of confusion among early breeders and fanciers. Needless to say, most Devon breeders did not participate in CFA shows because their cats would not fare well when judged or bred under that system. Finally, in 1979, the Cornish became known as Rex–Gene I and the Devon as Rex–Gene II, with two separate standards. In 1983, the Devon Rex was accepted for

Although the genetic difference between the two Rex breeds was clear in the early 1960s, the Cat Fanciers' Association did not recognize them separately until 1979.

Cornish Rex cats like these from Rexphiles Cattery are now bred in dozens of different colors and patterns—all with the same wonderful, curly coat.

championship status. It wasn't until 1984 that the CFA would change Rex into Cornish Rex as it is now known. Rex is now the term applied to all of the different curly-coated strains.

OTHER REX CATS

Other rex-coated cats have been found through the years. Karakul cats were known in the 1930s in the United States. Other known rex-coated breeds include the Oregon Rex, Ohio Rex, Colorado Rex, Tennessee Rex, Bohemian or Czech Rex, and Ural Rex. The Siamese Rex, or Si-Rex, was accepted by the CFA in 1985 as a Cornish Rex color. There are three long-haired rex-coated breeds as well: the California Rex (or Marcel), Selkirk Rex, and La Perm. There is even a line in England of rex-coated Maine Coons.

A German Rex called Lammchen, a black female, was discovered in 1951 in Berlin-Buch by Dr. Rose Scheuer-Karpin. The German Rex is genetically compatible with the Cornish Rex and has been absorbed into the Cornish Rex gene pool in the United States. Although rare, it can still be found as the German Rex in Europe. Its body type is interesting because it looks like a Devon Rex but is genetically the same as a Cornish Rex.

CHARACTERISTICS AND PERSONALITY

Cornish Rex are probably the friendliest cats you will ever meet. They will greet you or any guest who might come over at the door—especially if the new arrival is bearing food. It isn't unusual for visitors to walk into a house that has a Cornish Rex, only to discover the Cornish Rex sitting on their shoulders within minutes, meowing in their ears. They are extremely social cats that will howl and wail if there is a door separating them from their humans, the household activity, or the food.

Cornish Rex are probably the friendliest cats you will ever meet. They absolutely adore people—especially those bearing food.

Before selecting a Cornish Rex, make sure that an active, affectionate, playful cat is right for you.

Before selecting a Cornish Rex, you must first decide what you want in a cat. Do you want an elegant cat that will sit on your couch or at the foot of your bed looking decorative? Or do you want an active cat that will greet you when you come home and want to play with every possession you own? If it's the latter, the Cornish Rex just might be the cat for you.

HYPOALLERGENIC?

The Cornish Rex has received a lot of attention for being a hypoallergenic cat. Sadly for allergic cat lovers, no cat is truly hypoallergenic. Many people have found Cornish Rex to be the solution to their cat allergy problem, but others have found that they sneeze and sniffle around a Cornish Rex just as much as they do with any other cat. Please do your research before you buy a cat if cat allergies are what is prompting you to get a Cornish Rex. It would be heartbreaking to have to return that curly-coated cutie that you thought would be the answer to all your allergy problems after she had wrapped your heart around her skinny little paw.

Some breeders might offer you a "loaner" Cornish Rex for you to take home and "test-drive." This is not a good idea, because if you do find yourself to be allergic to the Cornish Rex, the allergens will be in your home where you will have to suffer from them for some time.

The best solution is to locate a Cornish Rex breeder that has no other types of pet, including cats, dogs, or birds. Some breeders have a special cattery set up for their Cornish Rex so that allergy sufferers can test their allergies without other allergic influences. Schedule a day when you can spend several hours with the Cornish Rex and do what you would want to do with your own cat, including petting, snuggling, or kissing. If after several hours you are allergy-free, you might have found yourself a new cat.

Some people find that although they are still allergic to the Cornish Rex, their reaction is sufficiently reduced that they can have one. Monthly baths for the cat in addition to a regular grooming regime can help the allergy situation. Allergy sufferers should also keep the cat's claws clipped to prevent bad scratches, which can cause severe allergic reactions. For some cat lovers, it

Despite the Cornish Rex's reputation as a hypoallergenic cat, some allergic cat lovers sneeze and sniffle around them just as with any other cat.

is worthwhile to invest in a high-efficiency particulate air (HEPA) filter and take antihistamines to help reduce allergic symptoms.

WHAT'S WRONG WITH THAT CAT?

A new Cornish Rex owner gets used to people asking, "What's wrong with that cat?" and "Is it supposed to look like that?" They have also been compared to space aliens with their large eyes and ears. Marian Babson described Cornish Rex in her 1972 mystery, *Murder at the Cat Show*, as "Strange, friendly, fantasy creatures, with curly astrakhan coats and great butterfly ears." Trina Schart Hyman, the illustrator for Marion Dane Bauer's 1992 book about an odd-eyed white Cornish Rex, *Ghost Eye*, called the Cornish Rex "an unbelievably hideous-looking animal." The Cornish Rex is a beautiful breed, and a cat with a lush, wavy coat will draw admiring cries from people—once they get used to her unusual appearance. Cornish Rex cats are such clowns that their personality is what usually wins over the skeptic and has converted many a dog lover into a cat person.

Above all, Cornish Rex cats are clowns that love getting attention for their antics.

Is it a space alien or is it a cat? It takes time to get used to the Cornish Rex's appearance, but their personalities win the hearts of everyone they meet.

INTELLIGENCE AND EXERCISE

Cornish Rex cats have high energy levels and therefore they

might not be the right breed for everyone. They love to race around the house and over and under furniture, regardless of knickknacks, people, or pets. They frequently get the "kitty crazies" and will go from napping to literally bouncing off the walls in no time flat. They love heights and can usually be found on top of the refrigerator, armoire, or door, peering down on life below—namely, we human floor-dwellers. Doorknobs are a challenge, and some Cornish Rex have discovered the secret of turning the knob. Doors with levers instead of knobs will be figured out promptly, and the Cornish Rex will get into the next room, the pantry, or outside. Many like to pick up small items in their paws and play soccer. Some can be trained to walk on a leash and go for a walk like a dog. Although most Cornish Rex slow down with age, they are still more active than other breeds in their prime.

A HARDY BREED

The Cornish Rex is a hardy breed, but it should not be subjected to extremes in temperature. Some people claim that the Cornish Rex should not be bred because it would freeze in extreme northern regions without a protective coat or jacket. The reverse argument could be applied to Persians or Himalayans in desert climates. The truth is that the Cornish Rex is a tough cat that only needs to

Cornish Rex cats love heights and can usually be found on top of the refrigerator, armoire, or door, peering down on life below.

have the same protection humans take when in extreme weather conditions. Simply provide your Cornish Rex with a warm bed or blanket and she will be happy.

White or light-colored Cornish Rex can get too much sun in southern climates or while sitting in windows, developing sunburns that can lead to skin cancer. It's a good idea to put sunscreen on cats that love to bask in the sun or to place ultraviolet (UV) screens in all sunny windows.

THE SENSITIVE CORNISH REX

Cornish Rex are extremely social cats and should never be left alone for long periods of time. Some breeders will sell two kittens at a discount so that they will each have a companion. Watching two or more Cornish Rex interact is one of the funniest experiences one can have in life. One cat fancier commented that she didn't have or need a television because she had Cornish Rex for entertainment.

Zeus, the one-year-old Cornish Rex on the right, snuggles in front of the fireplace with his buddy Shammy, a Devon Rex. Cornish Rex cats love to sleep in warm spots.

SELECTING A CORNISH REX

When selecting a Cornish Rex kitten, it is important to find a reputable breeder. The more you know about the history of the breeder and her cats, the more likely you will end up with a healthy kitten. Cat shows are a good place to start your search. Most breeders will be happy to answer questions if they are not busy grooming or showing their cat. You can also sit and watch the judge interact with the Cornish Rex cats as they are being shown. Are they bright-eyed and alert? Do they want to play?

Ask the breeder whose cats you like if she has a contract for buyers. Be wary of a breeder that does not have a contract, because that can show a lack of concern about the cat's welfare and future. Don't be insulted when you are asked to sign a contract. This shows that the breeder has the cat's best

It is important to find a reputable breeder who will sell you happy, healthy kittens like these 10-week-old Cornish Rex babies from Katkopelli Kats.

interests at heart, and the contract protects you in case of the kitten's illness or death.

Newspaper advertisements for Cornish Rex cats may come from kitten mills that try to crank out kittens as a source of income, with no concern about the kitten's health or longevity. (Also, even if the kittens *are* healthy, living conditions for the breeding parents may be truly abhorrent.) Again, ask a lot of questions. Pet stores are also not a good place to obtain a Cornish Rex, because the kitten might have traveled cross-country and you'll have no easy way to research the breeder.

THE QUALITY OF YOUR PET

You will generally be asked when buying a kitten if you want a pet, breeder, or show-quality kitten. Most breeders will only sell a pet-quality kitten to an unknown buyer. They usually want to see their top show-quality kittens go to a proven show home. Many will insist that you have previous experience showing either a household pet or a purebred premier if you wish to obtain a show kitten. That is one reason why it is a good idea to wait until a kitten is at least four months old, because at that age the breeder will have a better chance of evaluating the kitten's show potential. It also helps to find a mentor who will show you the ropes at the first couple of shows you attend.

Most breeders will want to sell their show-quality cats like odd-eyed van calico GC Blu Sprs Koko to proven show homes.

WHICH SEX TO PURCHASE?

Whether to get a male or female kitten is always a hard question. Because Cornish Rex tend to have more male kittens than female kittens, the males may be less expensive to purchase. Some people think that male cats bond more to women owners and female cats gravitate toward their male owners. It is usually less expensive to alter a male than a female Cornish Rex, because neutering is less invasive than spaying. Try not to go to the breeder with a definite sex in mind. Usually, one kitten out of a litter will choose *you*, which makes the decision easier for you.

WHAT AGE TO PURCHASE?

A reputable breeder will not sell a kitten that is younger than three or four months of age. Many people complain about receiving an older kitten, because they want something fluffy and cute

When you visit the breeder, it is likely that one kitten out of a litter will choose you, making your decision much easier.

and feel they have been cheated out of the kitten's babyhood. A reputable breeder knows, however, that a kitten younger than three months of age has not received all of her shots. The kitten also hasn't had a chance to learn proper social skills. Plus, many breeders will not sell a kitten less than four months of age because they cannot be shipped any younger than that. Don't feel cheated of the kitten's first few months, because your Cornish Rex will act like a kitten for the rest of her life.

There is a growing trend to alter the kitten before she leaves for her new home. There are several benefits to altering a kitten when she is so young. First of all, the breeder knows the surgery is being performed by a vet the breeder knows and trusts. It also ensures that the surgery is

A reputable breeder will not sell a kitten that is less than three or four months of age.

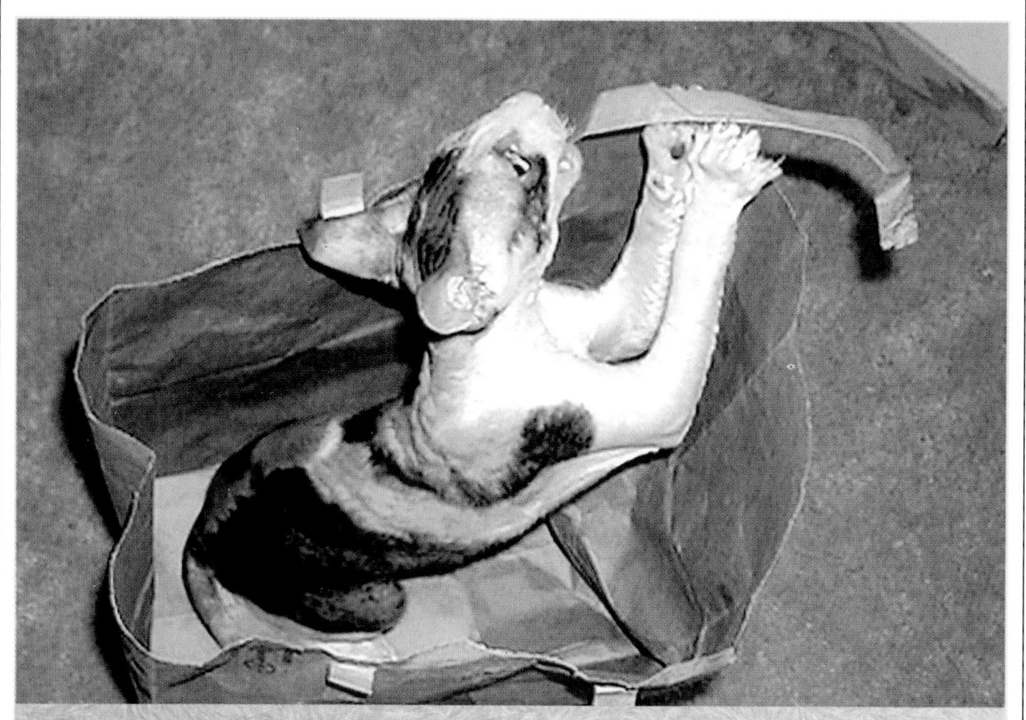

Although you are adopting an older kitten, remember that a Cornish Rex cat will be kittenish for life. Here, Quails Nest Melody Trail (age five months) demonstrates how much fun a paper bag can be.

done and prevents any accidental pregnancies and unwanted litters in the future. Finally, the new owner does not face the anguish and guilt in the event that the kitten dies during surgery. This tragedy *rarely* occurs, but when it does, it can be excruciating for the new owner.

ONE OR TWO CORNISH REX?

Cornish Rex are such friendly, social cats that it is a good idea to get two if there is no other cat or dog already at home to keep your new arrival company when you are not there. Many breeders will offer a discount if two kittens are purchased, because they want to see their kittens healthy and well socialized.

Cornish Rex are so friendly that it is a good idea to have another cat or dog to keep them company. Neelix, a Cornish Rex kitten, loves his Great Dane pal, Reno.

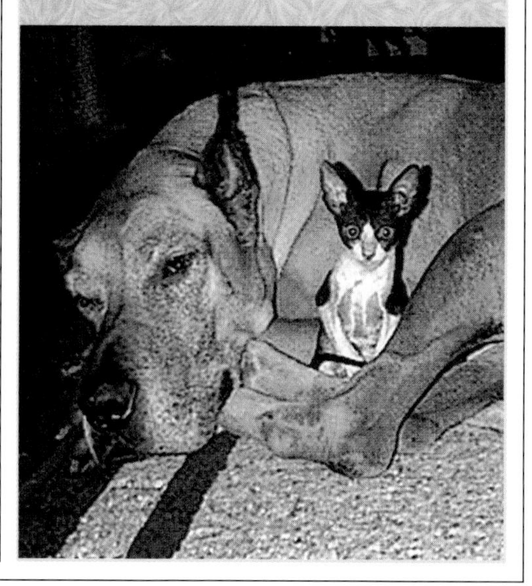

CHOOSING AN ADULT CORNISH REX

Choosing an adult Cornish Rex can be one of the most rewarding experiences a new owner can have. Many breeders have older retiring queens and studs that need loving pet homes as the breeder makes room for new additions to the cattery. This can be a real bargain, because most of these retirees are just 2 to 7 years of age, and a healthy, indoor Cornish Rex can live to be 15 years of age or more. Some breeders will even send the ribbons a retiring show cat has won to decorate your home.

Another wonderful way to get an adult Cornish Rex is to provide a loving home for a rescued Cornish Rex. Sadly, Cornish Rex cats occasionally need to be rescued when they have been abused, abandoned, or the previous owners have died without providing for their pets. If

Providing a loving home for an adult Cornish Rex cat like Cardell Vanessa of Rexphiles can be one of the most rewarding experiences a proud owner can have.

Which one (or two) will it be? Choosing a Cornish Rex cat or kitten can be lots of fun.

you are interested in a rescued Cornish Rex, try contacting the local humane society or rabies and animal control department to see if they will put you on a list. You might need to provide a photo and description of the Cornish Rex, because it is a rare breed and shelter workers might not even recognize one if it comes in. You can also contact local rescue groups to see if they will contact you if a rescued Cornish Rex becomes available. Finally, express your interest in a rescued Cornish Rex to your breeder. Most reputable breeders will help find homes for any rescued Cornish Rex they hear about. Many breeders and fanciers who believe in rescue work will post information on the Internet about known rescues.

Sometimes, a rescued Cornish Rex might have special physical or emotional needs that you will need to tend to. Many breeders are even pickier about the placement of their rescued Cornish Rex than their kittens because they do not want to see them dumped again. Many people become so addicted to Cornish Rex after experiencing their first that they turn to rescued Cornish Rex as a way to get more. It is a true joy to be the proud owner of a Cornish Rex that you know might have been euthanized if you had not given her a loving home.

GENERAL CARE AND GROOMING

The Cornish Rex is a breed that is easy to maintain. They don't require much grooming and are usually very healthy. They can be very stubborn, though, so decide early on what your Cornish Rex is permitted to do and then be consistent about it. One exasperated fancier once said that the plural for Cornish Rex should be a "persistence of rex"—similar to a pride of lions. He might have a point.

MYTHS AND OLD WIVES' TALES

If this is your first cat, you might have some worries or misconceptions caused by popular myths and old wives' tales. Cornish Rex are no exception to the potential harmful effects of these fabrications:

Cats do *not* always land on their feet, and many cats are injured or killed from falls out of windows or off balconies or roofs. The best solution is not to let

It's important to establish household rules from the start. Decide what your cat is permitted to do, and then be consistent about it.

Indoor cats like Winston, a rescued Cornish Rex, *can* get contagious diseases. Make sure to immunize your pet even if he never goes outside or to a cat show.

your Cornish Rex climb high places either inside or outside your home.

Cats should *not* drink milk because many cats are lactose-intolerant, which means they can get diarrhea from milk. There are milk substitutes on the market made just for cats that they can safely drink.

Cats do *not* gain weight because they are spayed or neutered. If your Cornish Rex is overweight, it's because her metabolism has slowed down, she is eating too much, or she is not getting enough exercise. Cornish Rex especially like to eat, so make sure your cat does not overeat and gets exercise.

Cats, like most warm-blooded mammals, *can* carry rabies. Cats should be vaccinated regularly just like dogs and according to local laws. Ask your veterinarian what the local laws are.

Indoor cats *can* get diseases through physical contact or even the air. That is why it is important to immunize your Cornish Rex even if she never goes outside or to a cat show. Visitors who own cats should wash their hands before handling your cats.

Tapeworms do *not* come from bad food but from fleas. Cats become infected with tapeworms from swallowing fleas that carry the parasite. Cats can also get tapeworms from eating infected mice or other animals.

Garlic will *not* get rid of worms. Your veterinarian can prescribe medicine if worms are detected.

Cats do use their whiskers as "feelers," but *not* to maintain their balance—which is a good thing, because so many Cornish Rex have very short whiskers.

Wounds will *not* heal faster if the cat licks them, so try to prevent your cat from licking any cut or wound, especially a surgical incision. It can actually slow the healing process and further damage the wound. Elizabethan collars are available to prevent your cat from hurting herself this way.

Cats do *not* suck the breath from babies. Any cat or dog should always be supervised around infants until the baby is old enough to turn herself over. Cornish Rex might find the baby to be a convenient sleeping surface because they like heat sources.

Wounds will not heal faster if the cat licks them—in fact, it can actually slow the healing process.

Pregnant women and people with suppressed immune systems *can* catch a disease from cats called toxoplasmosis, which can be spread to humans through cat litter boxes and can cause serious problems in unborn babies. Another family member or friend should do daily cleaning of litter boxes, but there is little or no risk from contact with the cat herself. A blood test is also available for the cat to see if she is a carrier.

ESSENTIAL SUPPLIES

Litter Box

Cornish Rex are by nature fastidious and require a clean litter box. The general rule is one litter box per cat. Most cats prefer the open boxes, because the hooded ones may contain bad odors. However, some cats like the privacy of a hooded litter box, so you might want to have at least one of each to see which kind your cat prefers. The litter you use is a matter of personal preference (both yours and the cat's). Some cats prefer the clumping kind, while others like the more traditional clay litter. There are also litters made from recycled newspaper, wheat, cedar, and citrus rinds. Do remember that your cat's preferences are more important than your own.

Many cats dislike the highly scented litters, so try to stick to the fragrance-free kinds. If you're unsure about the scent of the litter, put your nose next to a newly opened bag and sniff. If you think it smells too strong, think about what your cat must be smelling with her highly developed nose.

The type of cat litter can especially make a difference to a new cat. If she is used to scoopable litter, she might turn her sophisticated little nose up at clay and start using areas of your house that you never would have thought of as litter boxes. Check with the breeder about what the cat is used to and then gradually change the cat over to the type you prefer if you can. It is important to remember that very young kittens should not have access to scoopable litter, because they could inhale it or try to eat it, causing it to clump in their digestive systems. This is a problem with kittens that are learning to use the box—usually at around four weeks of age.

It is important to scrub the box out periodically. No matter how many times you change the litter, the sides of the tray will get grungy with time. Clay litter should be changed entirely once a week, and scoopable litter should be replaced at least once a month. Rinse the box very well after scrubbing it with a cleaning agent.

Scratching Post

Most people make the mistake of buying a post that is too short and are then surprised when the cat later refuses to use it. Try to get a scratching post that is at

Figlet and Digby love to relax atop their tall cat tree. A cat tree or scratching post that is at least 36 inches tall is best for adult Cornish Rex.

One of the best types of cat carriers is an approved plastic airline carrier like this one.

least 36 inches tall and place it in a spot where the cat will want to use it. Almost all cats will use a scratching post when the post is the right height, their claws are clipped, and a spray bottle is used to squirt the cat when she scratches in the wrong place.

Collar

Cat collars are optional, especially if your cat is kept strictly indoors. If you want to place a collar with a bell on your Cornish Rex so you always know where she is, use one of the breakaway collars so your cat can't get trapped and either hurt or kill herself trying to escape. Some people think that collars damage a Cornish Rex coat, but that depends on the quality of the cat's coat and how tight the collar is. You should be able to place three fingers between the cat and an appropriately fitted collar.

Cat Carrier

One of the best cat carriers is an approved plastic airline carrier. These carriers are sturdy, easy to clean, and come in various sizes to accommodate your cat's needs. Cardboard carriers are also available. They're cheap but they aren't sturdy, and many cats have escaped from them in transit.

Food and Water Dishes

If you see a dark, greasy-looking patch on your cat's chin, it's a good indicator of feline acne. Plastic dishes can cause feline acne, which is easy to spot on a Cornish Rex due to her short coat. Many cats are allergic to plastic, so you might want to provide metal or lead-free ceramic bowls for your cat's water and food dishes.

Brush

It is erroneous to say that Cornish Rex cats do not shed. They do shed, but not as much as most other breeds. A small amount of weekly brushing with a soft-bristled brush, a rubber brush, or your hand is usually all that is necessary. A piece of chamois, silk, or velvet is a wonderful way to burnish the Cornish Rex coat. It is important to groom your Cornish Rex regularly in the late spring because the breed does tend to shed its heavier winter coat when the weather warms up. Contrary to popular opinion, Cornish Rex can and do get hairballs. Provide your cat with a small amount of hairball remedy once a week to prevent them.

OPTIONAL SUPPLIES

Basket or Bed

Hooded and furry cat beds are popular with most Cornish Rex. Most will curl right up with the family dog or any other cats you might have, but a human lap is their bed of choice. The Cornish Rex will usually find the warmest spot in the house to sleep. That might be on top of a heat register, the refrigerator, or in a pile of warm laundry. Be careful when you turn on your dryer—more than one Cornish Rex has gone for a tragic ride inside the dryer. Most Cornish Rex are not content to sleep picturesquely at the foot of your bed. Many new Cornish Rex owners have been startled to find their cat crawling under the covers at night.

Cat Door

A cat door will not be needed if your Cornish Rex is kept inside,

Hooded and furry cat beds are popular with most Cornish Rex. Cannoli, however, can't seem to decide.

as she should be. Some people use cat doors to permit the cat to go out to an enclosed porch or into a closet that contains the cat's litter box.

Halter or Harness

A halter or harness is essential if a Cornish Rex is trained to walk on a leash. They are such agile monkeys that they can slip out of a collar and run before you know it. However, remove the halter or harness when it is not in use, because the cat can get caught on a rough surface and not be able to escape if she is wearing her harness.

All Cornish Rex need toys, whether they are expensive, store-bought toys or just a crumpled piece of paper.

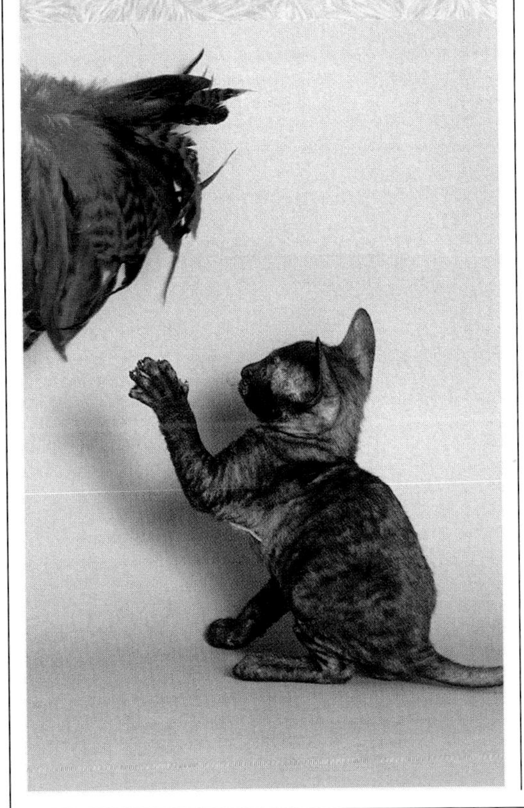

Toys

All Cornish Rex need toys. Pricey, store-bought toys are optional, but it really doesn't matter if they are expensive toys from a store or something homemade. Just remove any small parts that might come off and choke the cat or be swallowed, and never let a Cornish Rex play with a string or rope unsupervised. It could get wrapped around her neck and choke her.

CORNISH REX AND CHILDREN

The friendly nature of Cornish Rex cats makes them a natural pet for children. However, because of their small size, they can be hurt by rambunctious children. Make sure the kids are taught how to handle a cat. If the cat's claws are clipped regularly, the children will not get badly scratched by the cat if she is trying to defend herself.

CORNISH REX AND OTHER PETS

Cornish Rex are extremely friendly, social cats and generally get along well with other cats and dogs. When bringing home a new Cornish Rex, isolate her from the other pets until tests have proven the Cornish Rex is healthy and the animals get used to each other's scent. Because a Cornish Rex hates to be confined, she will usually make the first move toward exploring the rest of the house. Supervise these expeditions until you are sure that all the animals are comfortable with one another. They'll be sleeping in a cuddly pile together before you know it.

When your new Cornish Rex is introduced to your other pets, the fur may fly. However, they'll be sleeping in a cuddly pile like Kiksu and Piupiu before you know it.

SAFEGUARDING A CORNISH REX KITTEN

Just about the hardest aspect of owning a Cornish Rex kitten is baby-proofing your home all the way up to the ceiling. There is nothing too high or too small for a Cornish Rex to access, and you will find your cat stranded in the most unlikely places. Electrical wires also seem to be of great interest, so make sure all wires are tucked behind heavy furniture or in a paper towel tube where the kitten can't get to them too easily. Telephone cords can also be of interest to a curious Cornish Rex. One retired breeding cat made it her job to sever all the curly telephone cords she found. Costly abdominal surgery was required after she swallowed a section of cord. Cordless phones and retractable cords are now installed throughout her owner's house.

DISCIPLINE

The most important thing about discipline is to be consistent. Never hit your cat, because she will learn to fear you. Use a water squirt-bottle to spray the cat when she is doing something wrong. You can also place some pennies in a clean, empty soda can and tape the lid shut. Shake it to scare the cat when you see her misbehaving.

GROOMING

Bathing is hardly ever required unless your Cornish Rex got into something she wasn't supposed to or is getting ready for a show.

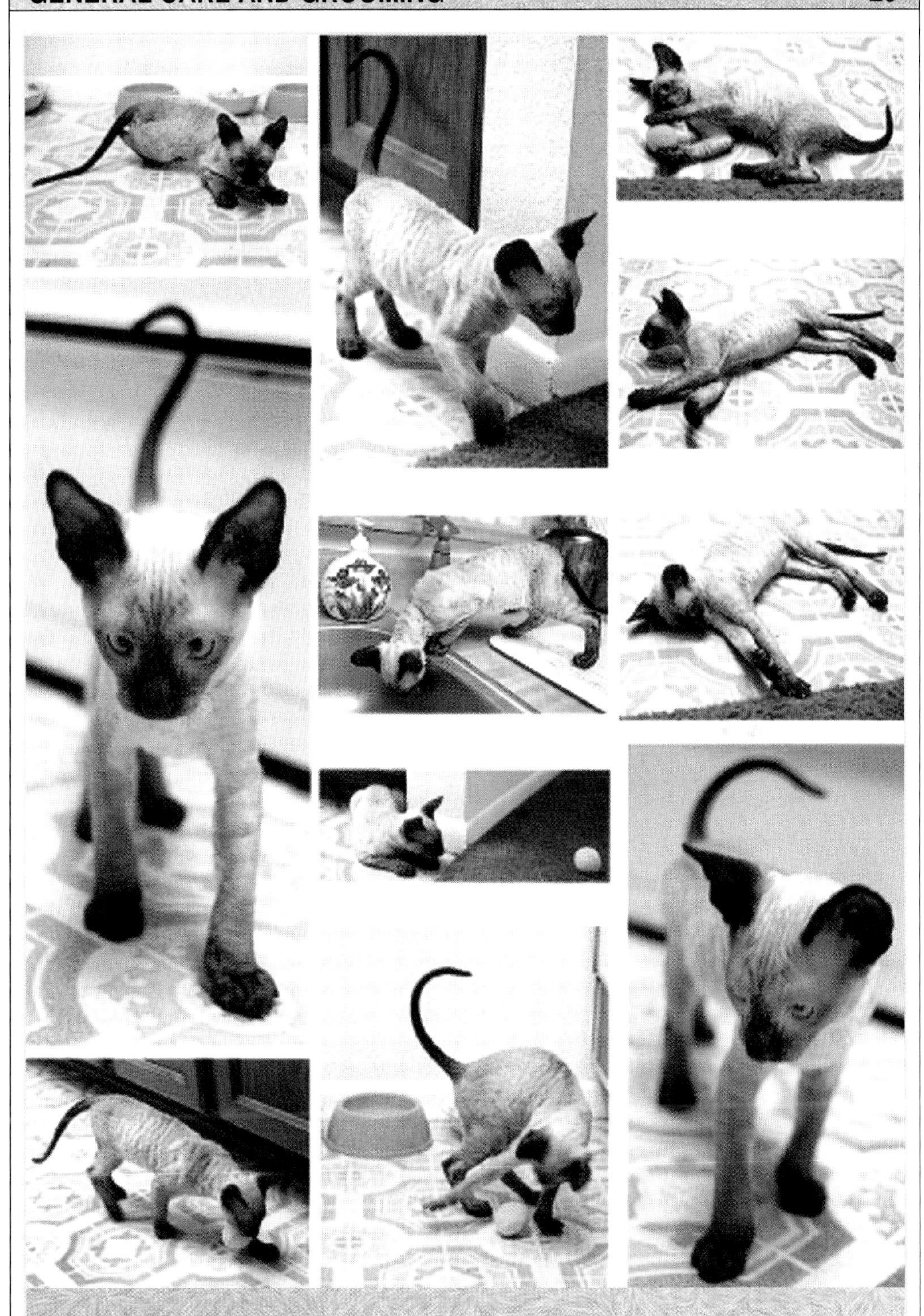

Crescent Kat Konfucius of Rexphiles, a three-month-old seal point Cornish Rex kitten, demonstrates the importance of baby-proofing your home. These little guys *never* stop moving.

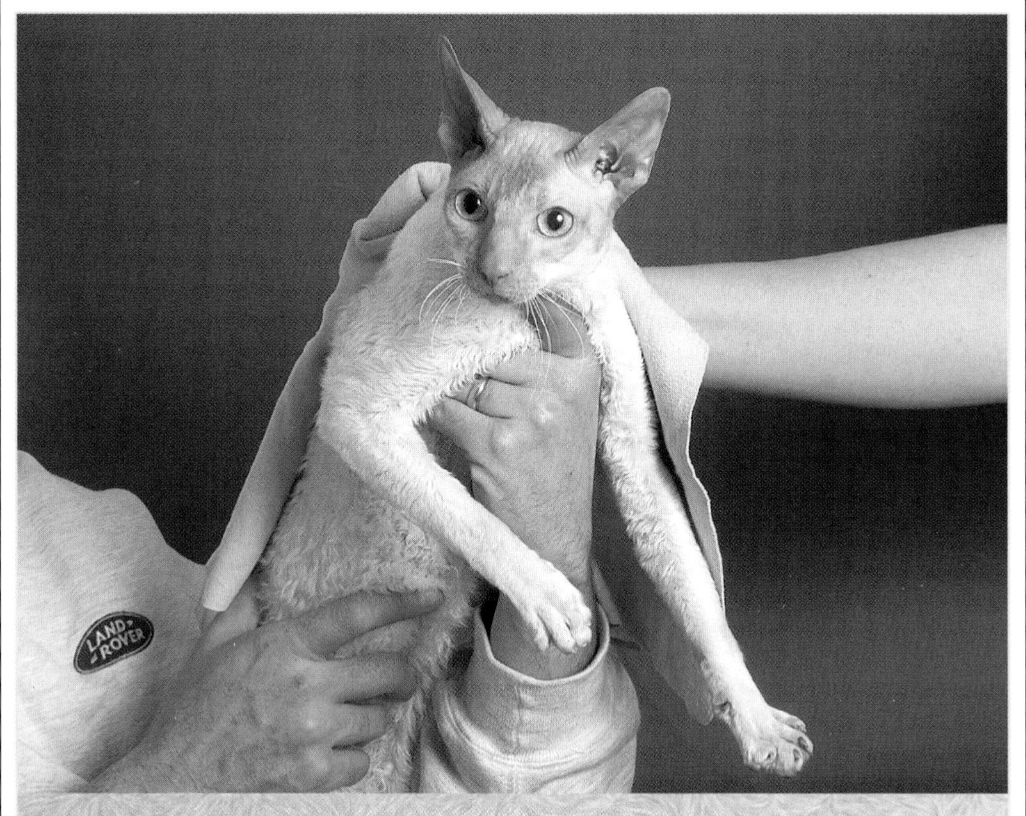

Cornish Rex cats rarely need a bath unless they are being prepared for a show.

The Cornish Rex coat can be damaged by too-frequent bathing or too harsh a shampoo, so be very careful in what you choose. Make sure the shampoo is formulated for cats only, because dogs and cats have different pH balances in their coats and skin. When bathing your cat, make sure you have everything ready before starting the bath. Most cats panic in a slippery tub or sink because there is nothing for them to hold onto. It is much easier on both you and your cat if you place a rubber mat or a window screen in the bathing area so the cat can sink her claws into the provided surface. Pour warm water over the cat, avoiding the face and ears. Usually, one lather and rinse is all that is necessary unless the cat is extremely dirty or greasy.

Rinse your Cornish Rex thoroughly, because you do not want the cat to ingest any chemicals when she grooms herself later. When you're done with the bath, wrap the cat in a warm, absorbent towel and gently dry the coat. Usually, a good hug will do it, because a Cornish Rex's coat is so short. Do not briskly rub the cat's fur with the towel because this can damage their coat. Stroking the cat with your hand as the cat is drying usually sets the waves in the right direction. You will have to discover

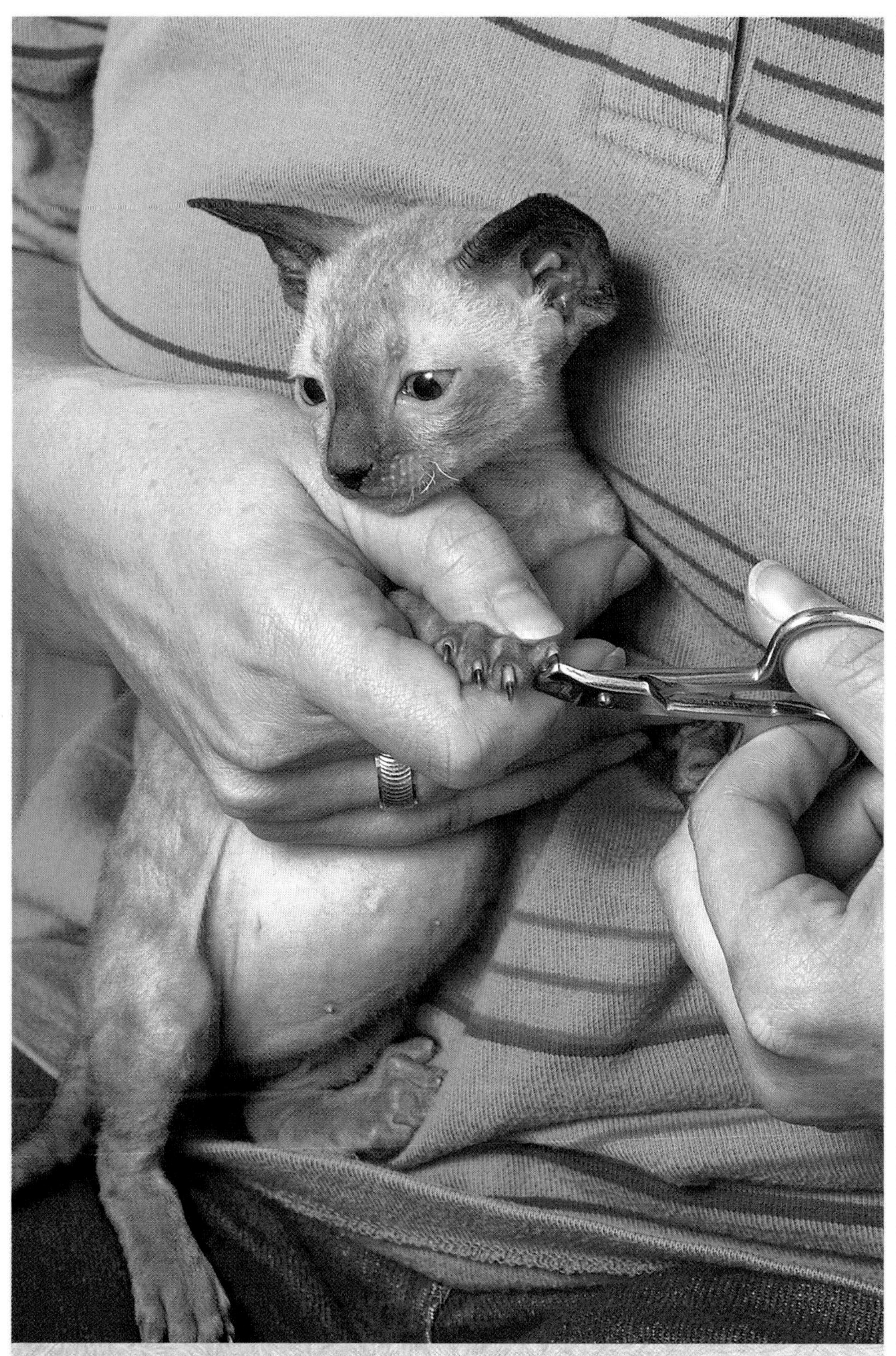

Your cat will get used to having her claws clipped if you start when she is very young.

through trial and error when it is best to bathe your cat before a show. Some Cornish Rex can be bathed the night before the show and look gorgeous, while others need about a week to recover the natural oils in their coats.

Some Cornish Rex have excessive earwax because they do not have the longer hair protecting their inner ears. This is sometimes mistakenly diagnosed as ear mites when it is simply a characteristic of the breed. It is a good idea to clean the outer ear of your Cornish Rex at least once a month, although once a week is better. If the buildup becomes too severe, the cat's ear may become red and infected.

It is a good idea to clean the outer ears of your Cornish Rex regularly, because some members of this breed have excessive earwax.

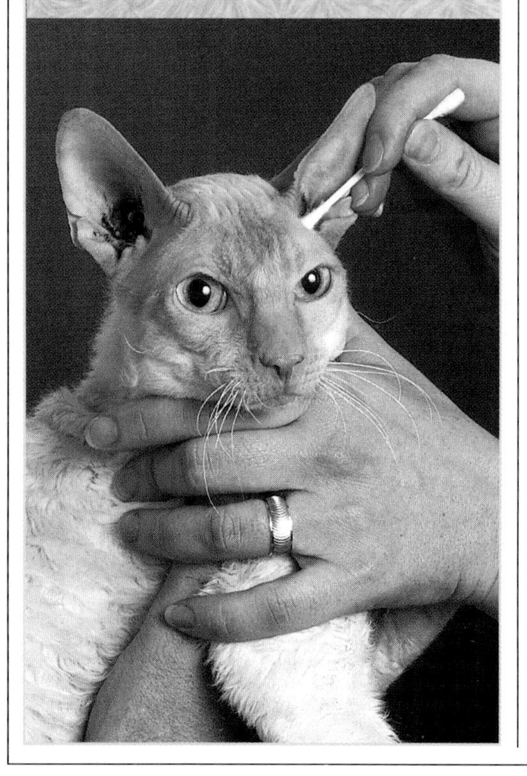

Never dig into the cat's ear canal, because you might damage the eardrum and cause your cat to become deaf. If the earwax is too deep, take the cat to your veterinarian for cleaning. A little ear-cleaning solution on a cotton ball swabbed around your cat's ear is usually enough to keep the cat's ears clean if this is done regularly. Massage the base of the ear after cleaning your cat's outer ear. The rubbing will help distribute any excess solution that dripped into the canal and help keep it clean.

Don't panic if you notice that your Cornish Rex has something that looks like blackheads on the top of her tail. That's exactly what they are, and this condition is called "stud tail." Male and female Cornish Rex can get this, especially those with a thinner coat. Regular bathing with a mild soap or acne medication can help ease this condition. If left untreated, the blackheads can infect and inflame the tail, making it uncomfortable for your cat.

When you clip your cat's claws, be sure to clip them as far down as possible without cutting the quick, which is the pink area visible toward the base of the nail. Don't remove just the tip of the claw, and remember to clip the claws on the hind feet too. Your cat will be used to this if you clip her claws at least once a month. If you are unsure how to do this, ask your veterinarian to show you.

FEEDING AND NUTRITION

Cornish Rex love to eat, and they will eat some of the strangest things. Therefore, it is very important to control the diet of your Cornish Rex kitten or cat. Otherwise, she will gain weight and lose that long and slender physique.

Cornish Rex love to eat, so it is important to control your cat's diet to keep her long and slender like Shal-mar's Sevilla of Rippleys, a smoke calico.

Although dogs can eat a carefully prepared vegetarian diet, cats must eat meat to survive. Dogs can also live on a cat-food diet, but cats will become ill on a purely dog-food diet. Cats need taurine, which is a nutrient found in poultry. Many cats became ill and died earlier in this century because of a taurine deficiency. Studies proved that cats needed this in their diet to remain healthy, so it is now a part of all complete cat foods.

COMMERCIAL FOODS

It is important to start off with a high-quality diet. While any cat food may provide the proper nutrition for your cat, the end results in the litter box can be very unappetizing. It pays in the long run to use a high-quality food that makes for a healthier cat and less waste and odor in the litter box.

The choice between wet and dry cat food is purely personal. Some people swear that dry food will keep the cat's teeth cleaner. It might help to some extent, but cats actually crush kibble against their hard palate instead of chewing it. Wet food is an alternative, especially for a cat that is having difficulty eating dry kibble. Some owners like to mix the wet and dry in equal portions. It is mostly up to you, although you might ask your veterinarian what to feed your cat if there are any medical needs.

If you do serve wet cat food, only put out a small amount at a time. If the cat doesn't eat it within 30 minutes, there is either too much in the dish or she doesn't like the food. Try a

The choice between wet and dry food is purely personal. Dry kitten food comes in smaller pieces than food made for adult cats.

smaller amount or a different brand next time. It is very important to wash the cat's dishes between meals or use paper plates if you serve wet food. That will prevent your cat from becoming ill from spoiled food and will help deter an ant invasion.

Dietary supplements are not necessary if the cat is eating a high-quality diet. One supplement that many Cornish Rex owners swear by is garlic and brewer's yeast. It can work wonders with the Cornish Rex coat by making it thicker, wavier, and healthier in appearance. It also works as a natural flea deterrent. Garlic and brewer's yeast comes in both powder and tablet forms. The powder can be mixed into the cat's food and the tablet can provide a crunchy treat.

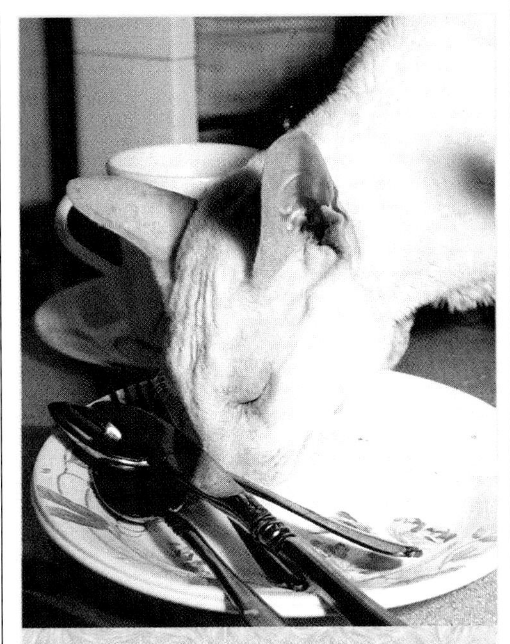

Like most cats, Crescent Kat Jesse Jms of Rexphiles will help himself to leftover "people food" whenever possible. Certain human foods, such as milk, poultry bones, and chocolate, can be dangerous to cats.

NON-COMMERCIAL FOODS

Cornish Rex as a breed love food, and the more the better. The tiniest sound in the kitchen will bring a Cornish Rex running from a nap that appeared to be a coma. If your Cornish Rex doesn't come running, it might be a sign that the cat is sick and needs to go to the veterinarian's office for a checkup. One of the breed's more unusual traits is that they love atypical foods such as vegetable juice, green beans, lettuce, coffee beans, and occasionally fruit.

Never give your Cornish Rex (or any other cat) cooked poultry bones. The cooking process makes the bones brittle and they will splinter when chewed. If your cat eats a splintered poultry bone, it could perforate the stomach or small intestine, leading to peritonitis and death.

HOW MUCH TO FEED?

Some people prefer to leave food out all day for their cat so she can eat as she wishes. However, free-feeding can lead to obesity for many Cornish Rex. Two small meals a day is what most Cornish Rex owners decide is the best way to keep the cat somewhat satisfied and still slim. It also helps the owner detect early warning signs of illness if the cat suddenly refuses or nibbles at food she has previously relished.

Some cats are fussy about their drinking water, so you might need to experiment with a different dish or source of water.

WATER

Fresh water is essential for your cat's health. Try to change the cat's water at least twice a day—more often if it gets contaminated. Some cats do not seem to drink water, so you might need to experiment with the type of dish or type of water (e.g., spring water, running faucet, etc.). The cat will not need to drink as much water if you are feeding her a wet-food diet. Some cats will not drink out of a plastic bowl, so you might try a steel or lead-free ceramic water dish. Other cats will only drink running water. There are small fountain water dishes now available for the cat that likes running water. The other option is to let the cat drink out of the faucets—but never let your cat drink out of the toilet. She could be poisoned by the cleaning chemicals. Also, many kittens have fallen into toilets and drowned. The best solution is to keep the seat and lid down and provide another source of water.

THE NEW ARRIVAL

When bringing your new Cornish Rex kitten or cat home with you, it is important to bring a supply of what that cat is used to eating or drinking home with you. A change of address is very traumatic for many cats, and the added stress of new food or water can be enough to make many cats ill with vomiting or diarrhea. If you plan on changing the brand of food your Cornish Rex is used to, do it slowly over a two-week period. Start off using mostly the old food and gradually add more of the new food until the transition is complete.

HEALTH CARE

Cornish Rex cats are a healthy breed and can live long lives if they are kept indoors and receive regular veterinary checkups and vaccinations. An outdoor cat has an average life span of about eight years. Cornish Rex can live to be 15 years of age or more if cared for properly. Some Cornish Rex have lived into their 20s. Regular brushing, claw clipping, and teeth cleaning is all that needs to be done at home for a healthy Cornish Rex.

Keeping your Cornish Rex indoors will help her stay healthy. If you insist on letting your pet go out, equipping your yard with a cat-proof fence or enclosure is mandatory.

RECOGNIZING AN ILL CAT

There are several ways to tell if your Cornish Rex is becoming ill. If you suspect your cat is ill, call the veterinarian immediately to discuss your concerns. Some things will heal themselves, but others can become critical if left for too long. It's best to err on the side of caution and consult with your vet when you have concerns.

Diarrhea is a sign of illness, especially if it is consistent or is accompanied by pus or a bloody discharge. It should also be cause for concern if the cat cries or strains when trying to defecate.

Vomiting can be another sign of poor health. Sometimes, it might be due to a hairball or new food, but constant vomiting should be reported to the vet immediately.

Any wheezing or congestion in the eyes, ears, or lungs should be reported to the vet. It might simply be a blocked tear duct or allergies, but it also might be an upper respiratory infection, which can be serious in both very young or old cats. Other signs are that the coat is looking dull and lifeless and the nictitating membranes are swollen and discolored.

Another sign is if your Cornish Rex refuses to eat. They have such hearty appetites that this is always suspicious. Call your veterinarian and discuss your cat's condition. Lethargy is also suspicious in a Cornish Rex.

Too much scratching can be a sign of fleas or other skin conditions. Call your vet if the

Because Cornish Rex are normally very active, persistent lethargy may be a sign of illness.

Too much scratching can be a sign of fleas or other skin conditions.

skin is becoming inflamed, red, or bloody.

When the cat scoots along the ground on her hindquarters, that can be a sign of impacted anal glands or a worm infestation. The veterinarian will need to be consulted.

VACCINATIONS

Cats are much more likely to be exposed to deadly diseases, not to mention fungal infections such as ringworm, if they are allowed to either go outside or socialize with a cat that is allowed outside.

Feline panleukopenia (FPV), feline viral rhinotracheitis (FHV-1), feline calicivirus (FCV), and rabies are so deadly that it justifies vaccinating all cats against these diseases. FPV is also known as feline distemper and feline infectious enteritis. The rabies vaccine is required in some states and is optional in others. Talk to your vet about local laws and about the local recommendations.

Rabies is an unknown disease on islands such as Hawaii, Great Britain, Australia, Japan, and Taiwan. These islands enforce strict quarantine laws to prevent rabies from entering. The only animals to receive a rabies vaccination are those that are leaving the island.

Vaccines against chlamydiosis, feline leukemia virus complex (FeLV), feline infectious peritonitis (FIP), and ringworm are optional. These vaccines should be limited to cats with a high risk of

Outdoor cats are much more likely to be exposed to deadly diseases. However, indoor cats should be vaccinated against these diseases as a precaution.

exposure. The effectiveness of FeLV and FIP vaccines has become so controversial in recent years that many breeders have a clause in the purchase contract stating that their kitten must not be vaccinated for these diseases.

Recent studies have shown that FPV, FHV-1, and FCV booster vaccines are only needed every three years for strictly indoor cats with limited exposure. They used to be recommended on a yearly basis. Cats that are boarded or that frequently go to cat shows may benefit from more frequent boosters.

Ringworm is actually a fungus and not a parasite, despite its name. Most breeders and fanciers don't bother using the ringworm vaccine as a preventive measure. They find it much more effective as a cure, in addition to some of the new oral prescriptions available. Contact your veterinarian if you see bald patches with thickened skin on your Cornish Rex. There are several tests that can be done to determine if it is ringworm or not. Ringworm can be cured and is never fatal except in very young kittens.

PARASITES

Cats or dogs that are allowed to go outside can pick up worms. Watch for white objects in the cat's feces. There are many

Young kittens are particularly susceptible to complications from ringworm. Contact your vet if you see bald patches with thickened skin on your Cornish Rex.

There are too many cats euthanized in the world, so neutering and spaying your Cornish Rex is a must if you don't plan to institute a careful breeding program.

medications available for treatment of these parasites. Heartworm is harder to detect and can be caught from mosquito bites. Ask your veterinarian about the local risk and if your cat should receive preventive medication. Most kittens are routinely treated for worms.

NEUTERING AND SPAYING

There are too many cats euthanized in the world, so neutering and spaying your Cornish Rex is a must if you don't plan on instituting a careful breeding program. When spaying and neutering became popular years ago, surgical anesthesia was not as safe as it is now, so the altering of very young kittens was discouraged until the kitten was six months old. (This is still the case in Great Britain.) Kittens are now frequently altered when they are 6 to 14 weeks of age. Cats that are not altered have a higher risk of cancer.

Remember that the Cornish Rex gene is recessive. Do not mate your Cornish Rex to the neighbor's sweet cat just because you like her looks or disposition and would like the same in your kittens. They won't be Cornish Rex kittens and can only be sold as ordinary kittens. There are no allowable outcrosses for the Cornish Rex. Some people have tried to sell "rare" Cornish–Devon Rex hybrid kittens. However, these are just plain old kittens instead of a unique rare breed.

A male that only has one testicle is called a monorchid. He will most likely be sterile and cannot be bred or shown unless it is as a neutered premier. There is also a chance that the undescended testicle is inside the cat's body cavity and will lead to a higher cancer risk. Get the male neutered and ask the veterinarian to locate and remove the other if present.

FIRST AID

Get your Cornish Rex to your veterinarian immediately if she is hurt, bloody, or unconscious. It is a good idea to place her on a rigid surface to prevent further injury and to wrap her in a blanket so she will not go into shock. Place direct pressure on any bleeding surfaces. Try to remain calm so you do not further upset the cat. It is a good idea to know where the nearest 24-hour emergency clinic is located, because cats frequently seem to wait until 3 a.m. to become ill or hurt. It is also a good idea to ask your vet what first aid items you should keep around for your cat. Never give your cat over-the-counter human drugs or prescriptions, including doses for children, without consulting the vet first. Many human drugs will kill a cat.

DECLAWING

Most cat registries will not allow a declawed cat to be shown, because many people believe that declawing is a cruel practice. Declawing, or onychectomy, is the removal of the cat's claw up to the first joint. A newer practice, called a tendonectomy, is the severing of the digital tendons, which prevents the cat from extending her claws. The claw is left on the cat in this case and must be clipped regularly so the claw will not grow full-circle

Instead of having your Cornish Rex declawed, which many breeders and other cat lovers believe to be cruel, clip your cat's claws regularly.

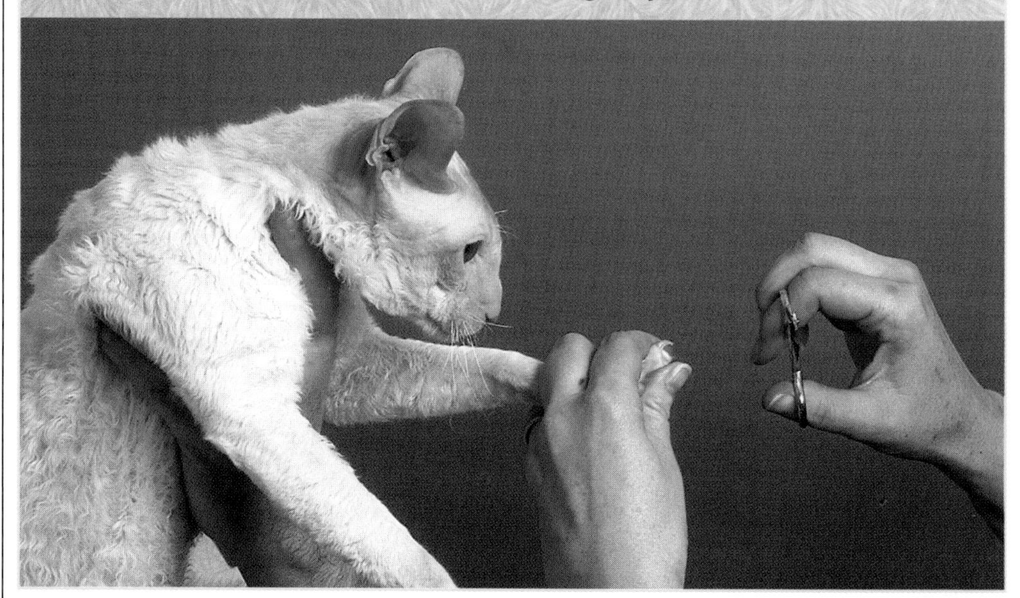

Special health concerns of the Cornish Rex include falsely diagnosed heart murmurs and accidental overdoses of preoperative sedatives.

and embed itself in the cat's paw. Go to the humane society or a rescue organization if you must have a declawed cat, because declawed cats regularly appear in those facilities.

SPECIAL BREED CONCERNS

Body Temperature

Because of their short coats, Cornish Rex cats feel warmer to the touch than ordinary cats. However, their body temperature is 101.5°F (38.6°C), just like all felines. A temperature that is higher than this indicates a fever.

False Heart Murmurs

For some reason, many veterinarians who are not familiar with the Cornish Rex may mistakenly hear a heart murmur. This has something to do with the shape of their ribcage. It is a good idea to get a second opinion if one veterinarian says there is a heart murmur. Try to find a veterinarian who has treated Cornish Rex before and is familiar with their needs and concerns.

Drug Overdoses

Another problem with the Cornish Rex is drug overdosing. Veterinarians who are not familiar with lean, exotic breeds will sometimes forget to adjust the dose of the prescription drug or the sedatives given before anesthesia. These "pre-ops" have

The veterinary sedative ketamine has caused several Cornish Rex to have strokes or neurological damage, and their recovery time from anesthesia is much longer than that of other cats.

recently been a topic of great concern among Cornish Rex fanciers and breeders.

Many veterinarians use a pre-op to sedate the cat before using the gas anesthesia during surgery. Due to the low body fat percentage in Cornish Rex, it can take weeks for the pre-op to work its way out of your cat's system. In the meantime, the cat will be wobbly. She may fall and hurt herself because she won't be used to this new sensation and will try to do her normal Cornish Rex thing. Some Cornish Rex have died from a pre-op overdose or suffered side effects such as deafness and brain damage. In particular, the veterinary sedative ketamine has caused several Cornish Rex to have strokes and neurological damage, and the recovery time from the anesthesia is much longer than in other cats.

Ask your vet to use the gas anesthesia without a preoperative sedative. It might cost more, but your cat will recover faster and thank you for it.

Topical preventive flea medications can usually be used safely if adjusted for the Cornish Rex's lower weight. Have your veterinarian research the specific product for any data available on use with lean breeds like the Cornish Rex. Most Cornish Rex fall into the kitten category in medication dosages.

STANDARD AND COLORS OF THE CORNISH REX

As previously mentioned, the owner of a Cornish Rex gets used to people asking, "What's wrong with that cat?" That was even a line in the 1991 movie *F/X 2,* when Brian Dennehy's character asked a woman about her Cornish Rex. Admittedly, the Cornish Rex does look a bit different from most other breeds. It has a small, egg-shaped head with large eyes, high cheekbones, and a Roman nose. The head is topped with large ears that are set high on the head. The small to medium-sized body is deceptively heavy, with its full chest, arched back, defined waist, long, lean legs, and whiplike tail. Those same legs have well-developed muscles that make running, leaping, and

The Cornish Rex has a small, egg-shaped head with large eyes, high cheekbones, and a Roman nose. The ears are large and set high on the head.

THE CORNISH REX STANDARD

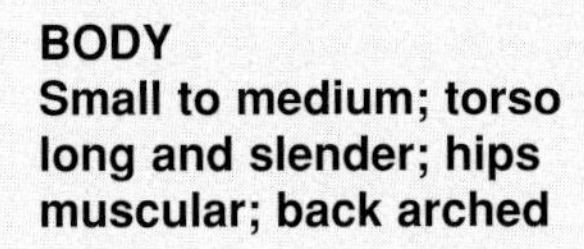

COAT
Short, soft, silky, dense, no guard hairs; tight, uniform marcel wave

RUMP
Rounded, well-muscled

TAIL
Long and slender, tapering

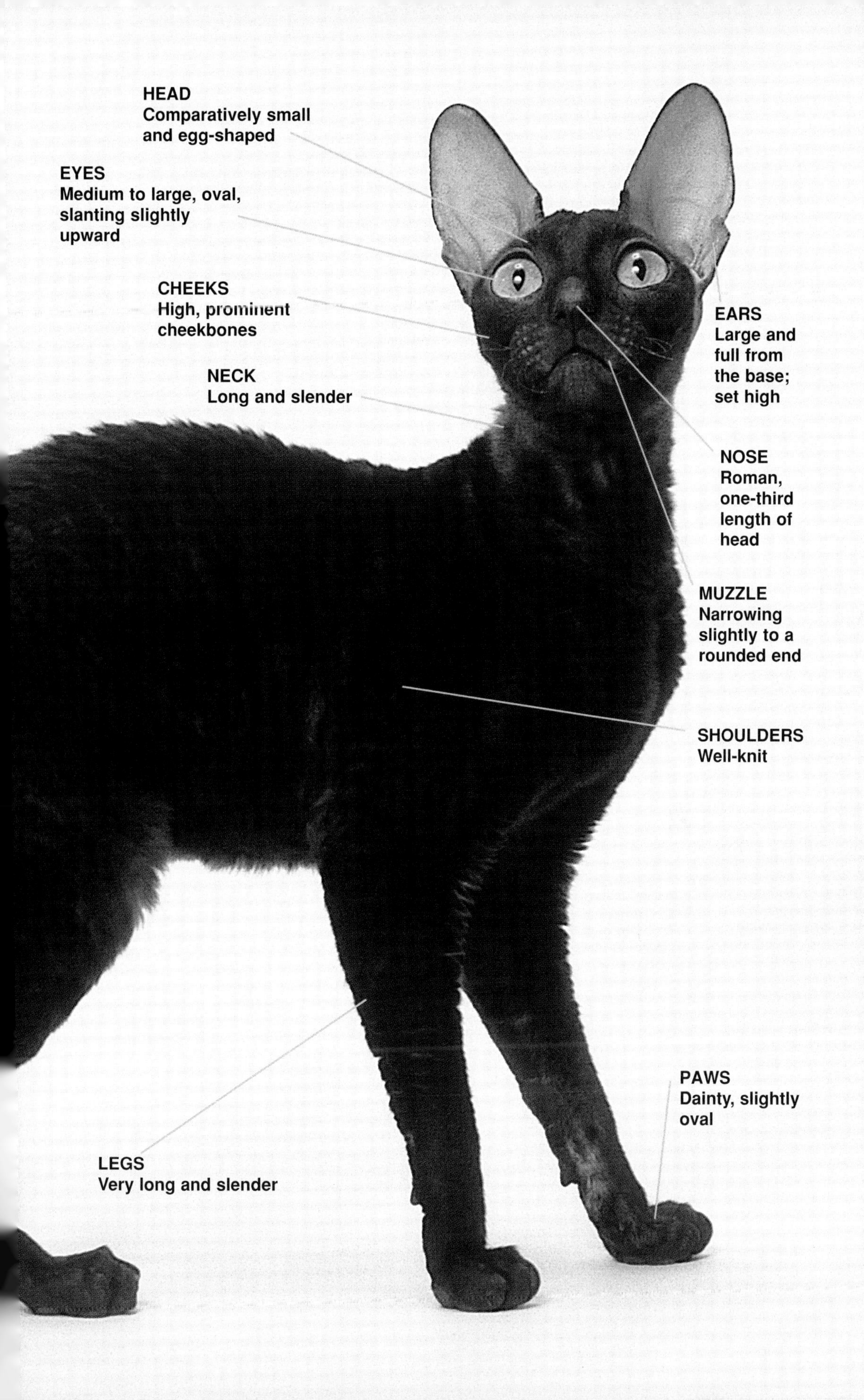
HEAD
Comparatively small and egg-shaped
EYES
Medium to large, oval, slanting slightly upward
CHEEKS
High, prominent cheekbones
NECK
Long and slender
EARS
Large and full from the base; set high
NOSE
Roman, one-third length of head
MUZZLE
Narrowing slightly to a rounded end
SHOULDERS
Well-knit
PAWS
Dainty, slightly oval
LEGS
Very long and slender

sharp turns possible for this energetic breed.

But what is it that makes the Cornish Rex different from other breeds? There has always been debate about that. Is it the curly coat, the lithe body, or the outgoing personality? Some say it is one or the other, while others say that it is all three. The coat is certainly an identifying feature of the Cornish Rex breed. Most breed coats are made of three layers of fur: the coarse outer guard hairs, the inner awn hairs, and the fluffy undercoat. The Cornish Rex coat only has the undercoat, which is why it is so soft to the touch.

ABOUT BREED STANDARDS

Because the Cornish Rex is so different from other cats in appearance, it is especially important to have a standard for fanciers, breeders, and judges to follow. A standard is used to compare the cat in question with the ideal example of the breed: Does this cat have a Roman nose? Does she have a curly coat? Does she have an elegant, lean body? Does she have any faults, such as a kinked tail? These questions must all be answered when trying to judge the ideal Cornish Rex. If the cat has a nice, egg-shaped head but the ears are small and set low, then that Cornish Rex would make a wonderful pet but should not be shown or used for breeding.

THE CORNISH REX STANDARD

As of May 21, 1999, the Cornish Rex breed standard, according to

The torso of a Cornish Rex should be long and slender but not tubular.

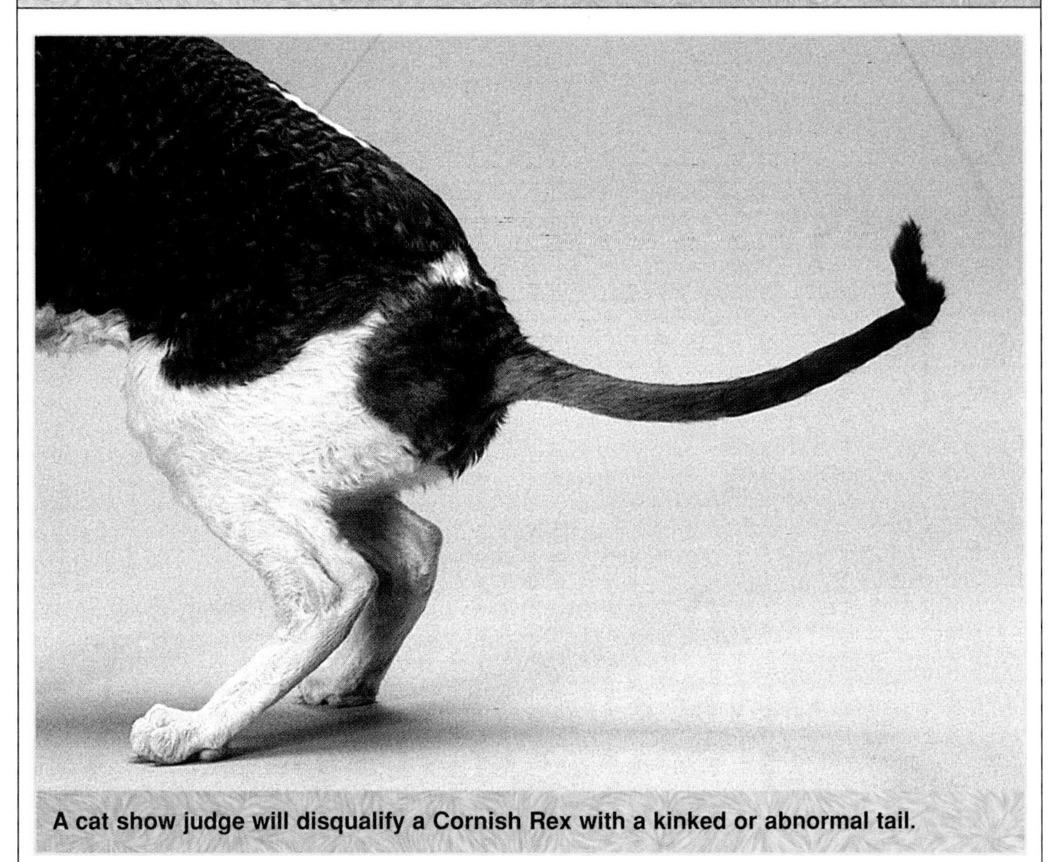

A cat show judge will disqualify a Cornish Rex with a kinked or abnormal tail.

the CFA, is as follows. It is reprinted here with permission.

General: The Cornish Rex is distinguished from all other breeds by its extremely soft, wavy coat and racy type. It is surprisingly heavy and warm to the touch. All contours of the Cornish Rex are gently curved. By nature, the Cornish Rex is intelligent, alert, and generally likes to be handled.

Profile: A curve comprised of two convex arcs. The forehead is rounded, the nose break smooth and mild, and the Roman nose has a high prominent bridge.

Head: Comparatively small and egg shaped. Length about one-third greater than the width. A definite whisker break, oval with gently curving outline in front and in profile.

Muzzle: Narrowing slightly to a rounded end.

Ears: Large and full from the base, erect and alert; set high on the head.

Eyes: Medium to large in size, oval in shape, and slanting slightly upward. A full eye's width apart. Color should be clear, intense, and appropriate to coat color.

Nose: Roman. Length is one-third length of head. In profile a straight line from end of nose to chin with considerable depth and squarish effect.

Cheeks: Cheek bones high and prominent, well-chiseled.

Chin: Strong, well-developed.

Body: Small to medium, males proportionately larger. Torso long and slender, not tubular; hips, muscular and somewhat heavy in proportion to the rest of the body. Back is naturally arched with lower line of the body approaching the upward curve. The arch is evident when the cat is standing naturally.

Shoulders: Well-knit.

Rump: Rounded, well-muscled.

Legs: Very long and slender. Thighs well-muscled, somewhat heavy in proportion to the rest of the body. The Cornish Rex stands high on its legs.

Paws: Dainty, slightly oval. Toes: five in front and four behind.

Tail: Long and slender, tapering toward the end and extremely flexible.

Neck: long and slender.

Bone: Fine and delicate.

Coat: Short, extremely soft, silky, and completely free of guard hairs. Relatively dense. A tight, uniform marcel wave, lying close to the body and extending from the top of the head across the back, sides, and hips, continuing to the tip of the tail. Size and depth of wave may vary. The fur on the underside of the chin and on chest and abdomen is short and noticeably wavy.

Condition: Firm and muscular.

Penalize: Sparse coat or bare spots.

Disqualify: Kinked or abnormal tail. Incorrect number of toes. Any coarse or guard hairs. Any signs of lameness in the hindquarters. Signs of poor health.

Cornish Rex Colors

White: Pure glistening white. *Nose leather and paw pads:* pink. *Eye color:* deep blue or brilliant gold. Odd-eyed whites shall have one blue and one gold eye with equal color depth.

Black: Dense coal black, sound from roots to tip of fur. Free from any tinge of rust on the tips. *Nose leather:* black. *Paw pads:* black or brown. *Eye color:* gold.

Blue: Blue, lighter shade preferred, one level tone from nose to tip of tail. Sound to the roots. A sound darker shade is more acceptable than an unsound lighter shade. *Nose leather and paw pads:* blue. *Eye color:* gold.

Red: Deep, rich, clear, brilliant red; without shading, markings, or ticking. Lips and chin the same color as the coat. *Nose leather and paw pads:* brick red. *Eye color:* gold.

Cream: One level shade of buff cream, without markings. Sound to the roots. Lighter shades preferred. *Nose leather and paw pads:* pink. *Eye color:* gold.

Chinchilla silver: Undercoat pure white. Coat on back, flanks, head, and tail sufficiently tipped with black to give the characteristic sparkling appearance. Legs may be slightly shaded with tipping. Chin, stomach, and chest, pure white. Rims of eyes, lips, and nose outlined with black. *Nose leather:* brick red. *Paw pads:* black. *Eye color:* green or blue-green.

Shaded silver: Undercoat white with a mantle of black tipping shading down from sides,

The intelligent, alert, and friendly nature of the Cornish Rex is an important part of the breed's standard.

face, and tail from dark on the ridge to white on the chin, chest, stomach, and under the tail. Legs to be the same tone as the face. The general effect to be much darker than a chinchilla. Rims of eyes, lips, and nose outlined with black. *Nose leather:* brick red. *Paw pads:* black. *Eye color:* green or blue-green.

Black smoke: Individual hair shafts white, each deeply tipped with black. In repose, the cat appears black. In motion, the white base of the hairs is readily apparent. Points and mask black with narrow band of white at base of hairs next to skin which may be seen only when fur is parted. *Nose leather and paw pads:* black. *Eye color:* gold.

Blue smoke: Individual hair shafts white, each deeply tipped with blue. In repose, the cat appears blue. In motion, the white base of the hairs is readily apparent. Points and mask blue with narrow band of white at base of hairs next to skin which may be seen only when fur is parted. *Nose leather and paw pads:* blue. *Eye color:* gold.

Classic tabby pattern: Markings dense, clearly defined, and broad. Legs evenly barred with bracelets coming up to meet the body markings. Tail evenly ringed. Several unbroken necklaces on neck and upper chest, the more the better. Frown marks on forehead form an intricate letter "M." Unbroken line runs back from outer corner of eye. Swirls on cheeks. Vertical lines over back of head extend to shoulder markings which are in the shape of a butterfly with both upper and lower wings distinctly outlined and marked with dots inside outline. Back markings consist of a vertical line down the spine from butterfly to tail with a vertical stripe paralleling it on each side, the three stripes well separated by stripes of the ground color. Large solid blotch on each side to be encircled by one or more unbroken rings. Side markings should be the same on both sides. Double vertical rows of buttons on chest and stomach.

Mackerel tabby pattern: Markings dense, clearly defined, and all narrow pencilings. Legs evenly barred with narrow bracelets coming up to meet the body markings. Tail barred. Necklaces on neck and chest

Ch. Twizzler Spot Luck of Apple Lake, a brown mackerel tabby and white Cornish Rex.

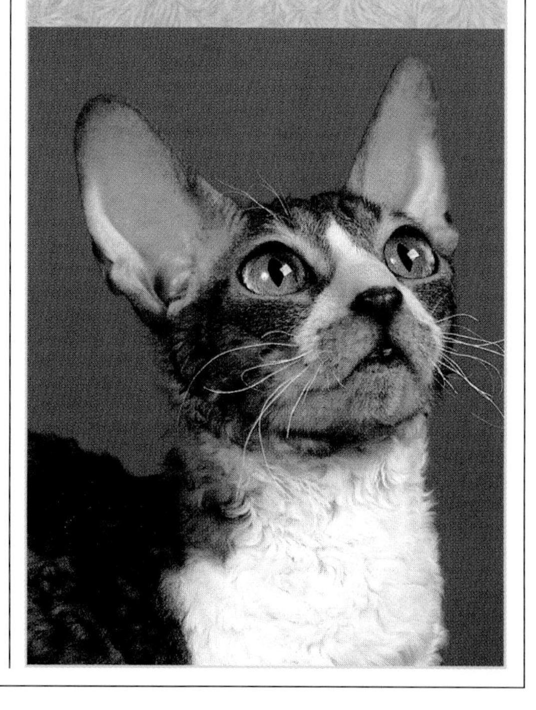

distinct, like so many chains. Head barred with an "M" on the forehead. Unbroken lines running back from the eyes. Lines running down the head to meet the shoulders. Spine lines run together to form a narrow saddle. Narrow pencilings run around body.

Patched tabby pattern: A patched tabby (torbie) is an established silver, brown, or blue tabby with patches of red and/or cream.

Brown patched tabby: Ground color brilliant coppery brown with classic or mackerel tabby markings of dense black with patches of red and/or cream clearly defined on both the body and extremities; a blaze of red and/or cream on the face is desirable. Lips and chin the same shade as the rings around the eyes. *Eye color:* brilliant gold.

Blue patched tabby: Ground color, including lips and chin, pale bluish ivory with classic or mackerel tabby markings of very deep blue affording a good contrast with ground color. Patches of cream clearly defined on both body and extremities; a blaze of cream on the face is desirable. Warm fawn overtones or patina over the whole. *Eye color:* brilliant gold.

Silver patched tabby: Ground color, including lips and chin, pale silver with classic or mackerel tabby markings of dense black with patches of red and/or cream clearly defined on both body and extremities. A blaze of red and/or cream on the face is desirable. *Eye color:* brilliant gold or hazel.

Silver tabby (classic, mackerel): Ground color, including lips and chin, pale clear silver. Markings dense black. *Nose leather:* brick red. *Paw pads:* black. *Eye color:* green or hazel.

Red tabby (classic, mackerel): Ground color red. Markings deep, rich red. Lips and chin red. *Nose leather and paw pads:* brick red. Eye color: gold.

Moire Crash Landing, a red tabby Cornish Rex.

Brown tabby (classic, mackerel): Ground color brilliant coppery brown. Markings dense black. Lips and chin the same shade as the rings around the eyes. Back of leg black from paw to heel. *Nose leather:* brick red. *Paw pads:* black or brown. *Eye color:* gold.

Blue tabby (classic, mackerel): Ground color, including lips and chin, pale bluish ivory. Markings a very deep blue affording a good contrast with ground color. Warm fawn overtones or patina over the whole. *Nose leather:* old rose. *Paw pads:* rose. *Eye color:* gold.

Cream tabby (classic, mackerel): Ground color, including lips and chin, very pale cream. Markings buff or cream sufficiently darker than the ground color to afford good contrast but remaining within the dilute color range. *Nose leather and paw pads:* pink. *Eye color:* gold.

Tortoiseshell: Black with patches of red or softly intermingled areas of red on both body and extremities. Presence of several shades of red acceptable. Blaze of red on face is preferred. *Nose leather and paw pads:* black and/or brick red. *Eye color:* gold.

GC Blu Sprs Koko, an odd-eyed van calico Cornish Rex.

Tortoiseshell smoke: Individual hair shafts white, each deeply tipped with red or black. In repose, cat appears tortoiseshell. When the coat is parted, the white base of the hairs is readily apparent. Points of the cat may exhibit deeper tipping than in the rest of the coat. *Nose leather and paw pads:* black and/or brick red. *Eye color:* gold.

Calico: White with unbrindled patches of black and red. White predominant on underparts. *Eye color:* gold, odd-eyed, or blue.

Calico smoke: White with unbrindled patches of black and red. Non-white areas have a white undercoat, deeply tipped with black or red. Cat in repose appears calico. When the coat is parted, the undercoat is clearly apparent. Points of the cat may exhibit deeper tipping than in the rest of the coat. *Eye color:* blue, gold, or odd-eyed.

Van calico: White cat with unbrindled patches of black and red confined to the extremities; head, tail and legs. One or two small colored patches on body allowable. *Eye color:* gold, blue, or odd-eyed.

Dilute calico: White with unbrindled patches of blue and cream. White predominant on underparts. *Eye color:* gold, blue, or odd-eyed.

GC, RW Heatwave The Wind Beneath My Wings, a dilute calico Cornish Rex.

Blue-cream: Blue with patches of solid cream. Patches clearly defined and well broken on both body and extremities. *Eye color:* gold.

Dilute van calico: White cat with unbrindled patches of blue and cream confined to the extremities; head, tail, and legs. One or two small colored patches on body allowable. *Eye color:* gold, blue, or odd-eyed.

Bicolor: Solid color and white, smoke and white, tabby and white, etc. Cats with no more white than a locket and/or button do not qualify for this color class. Such cats shall be judged in the color class of their basic color with no penalty for such locket and/or button. *Eye color:* gold, odd-eyed, or blue.

Van bicolor: Black and white, red and white, blue and white, cream and white. White cat with color confined to the extremities; head, tail, and legs. One or two small colored patches on body allowable. *Eye color:* gold, blue, or odd-eyed.

ORC (Other Rex Colors): Any other color or pattern. *Eye color:* appropriate to the predominant color of the cat. Eye color (where any other color or pattern is coupled with white, exclusive of buttons or lockets): gold, blue, or odd-eyed. The point system used by CFA is as follows. Notice that the coat is the area earning the highest points.

Point Score of the CFA

Head (25)

Size and shape	5
Muzzle and Nose	5
Eyes	5
Ears	5
Profile	5

Body (30)

Size	3
Torso	10
Legs and Paws	5
Tail	5
Bone	5
Neck	2

Coat (40)

Texture	10
Length	5
Wave, Extent of Wave	20
Close Lying	5

Color (5)

There are no allowable outcrosses in the Cornish Rex breed.

In the CFA standard, the Cornish Rex's coat is the most important single element of the breed and is worth 40 out of 100 possible points.

Vildarex Valmont, a black smoke/white van bicolor Cornish Rex premier.

EXHIBITING THE CORNISH REX

Showing your Cornish Rex kitten or cat can be a lot of fun. It can also be addictive and very expensive. The first problem can be deciding if your Cornish Rex is show-quality or not. Especially because of the breed's endearing personality, nearly everyone thinks their Cornish Rex is a winner.

TYPES OF SHOWS

Shows are either all-breed or specialty. In an all-breed show, all cats compete for various awards regardless of coat length or type. In a specialty show, only those cats of similar coat length or type compete.

ENTERING A SHOW

If possible, attend a few shows first as a spectator. This will give you an idea of what to expect and what goes on at a show. Then order a copy of the show rules and study them carefully if you are still interested. The show rules contain important facts about entry eligibility, entry procedures, and the responsibilities of exhibitors. The standard for the Cornish Rex, which is contained in this book, will also need to be studied.

Show listings, show locations, entry fees, and the name, address, and telephone number of the entry clerk are presented several months in advance in various cat publications and the various cat registry Web sites. Select the show you want to attend and request a show flyer and an entry form for each cat entered in the show. Some clubs will offer an "early bird" entry fee, but all shows have a closing date for entries. It is a good idea to get a double cage if you are given the choice. It will give both you and your cat more room to relax for only a small additional fee. You can also request if you want to be benched with your mentor or others showing the same breed. Send in your completed entry form and the entry fee before the

Before deciding to show your Cornish Rex, determine whether she is show-quality or not. GC Roseric's Getn' Some Nooky Tonite definitely has that special something.

specified closing date when you have decided which show you want to attend. Call the entry clerk only if you do not receive verification that you've entered the show or have questions that a more experienced exhibitor can't answer for you.

THE DAY OF THE SHOW

Take your verification with you when the day of the show arrives and allow ample travel time prior to check-in. Make sure you transport your Cornish Rex in a safe carrier so it doesn't escape in the confusion.

It is a good idea to arrive at the show hall at least one hour before the judging starts. Check in with the entry clerk when you arrive, who will give you a cage number and benching row designation. Then locate your cage, set it up, and clean it, because many cat clubs do not clean the cages between shows. A spray-bottle of weak bleach solution (1 part bleach to 30 parts water) will do the job nicely. A fresh solution will need to be made every day of the show, because it will lose its disinfecting ability after 24 hours. Let everything dry thoroughly before decorating and placing your cat in the cage. Many breeders bring their own cages, including some that lock, to prevent any contamination or theft.

It's a good idea to attend a few cat shows first as a spectator. This will give you an idea of what to expect.

When you arrive at the show hall, you will first need to set up your cage. Here, Norma Berke and her black smoke Cornish Rex Figment's Jessie Norman demonstrate the finished product.

SHOW CAGES

Show curtains or some kind of drape such as a sheet or towel are needed to provide your cat with a sense of privacy and security. They also prevent unaltered males from spraying each other and helps keep the yowling to a minimum. It is nice to choose curtains that will showcase your cat's colors and reflect your cattery's name if you have one. It can also be fun to have curtains that will reflect the cat show's theme or an upcoming holiday. Washable curtains are a great idea in case your cat gets sick or sprays them. Fancy satin curtains can be beautiful but are more expensive to clean and maintain.

Once you have put up your show curtains and before placing the cat in her cage, add items that might make your Cornish Rex feel at home such as a favorite toy, a bed to sleep on, her favorite dishes, and her litter box. Some shows will provide food and litter, but many exhibitors prefer to bring their own. The more you can provide your cat that is known and familiar, the happier the cat will be. But don't worry if she doesn't eat, because she is probably just nervous and will eat when she is back home.

After setting up the cage, it is very important to check the judging schedule and locate each ring so that you won't be late or miss your cat's judging call.

There is a lot of time spent between judging when you can tour the show, see all the different breeds, and talk with their owners. Never touch another cat unless invited by the owner. Diseases are easily spread by contact, and you don't want to make either your cat or the other exhibitors' cats sick. It's always a good idea to make friends with your neighbors, especially if they are not your mentor, because they can watch your cat when you're away from the benching area. Do not hesitate to ask questions if they are not busy. They will be happy to discuss their cats with you.

MISCELLANEOUS ITEMS

You will want your cat to look his best during judging, so bring a soft-bristled brush, rubber brush, chamois, or a piece of silk or velvet to touch up the coat of your Cornish Rex. Claw clippers are also a good thing to have to loan to people who have forgotten theirs at home. Show rules demand that cat claws be clipped, and cats whose claws haven't been clipped may be refused entry.

When showing, it is important to take along items that will keep both you and your Cornish Rex comfortable. Some necessary items are pens and sign materials, paper clips or pipe cleaners to wire shut a loose door or to use for hanging signs, business cards, newspapers or carpet samples for lining the cage, antibacterial hand cleanser for spectators who want to touch your cat, paper bags for disposing of trash, articles about the Cornish Rex, and a sweater and socks in case the show hall is chilly. You'll also need something in which to carry everything. Don't make more trips to the car than you absolutely have to.

JUDGING

A cat show is composed of many individual shows held in the various judging rings throughout a show hall. Each show is presided over by a different judge, who presents awards without the influence of other judges. A cat that is chosen

Each ring at a cat show is presided over by a different judge.

Best in Show by the judge in Ring One may not even place with the judge in Ring Two.

SHOW CLASSES

The CFA does not permit declawed cats in any of its six categories.

Kitten competition is for unaltered or altered pedigreed kittens between the ages of four and eight months of age.

Championship competition is for pedigreed cats over the age of eight months that have not been spayed or neutered.

Premiership competition is for pedigreed cats over the age of eight months that have been spayed or neutered.

Provisional competition is for new or experimental breeds that have not yet achieved championship status. This class is the final step before a breed is accepted for championship competition. Cats in the provisional class compete up to the best of breed award but are not eligible for finals until the breed is advanced to championship status.

Miscellaneous competition puts a breed on exhibition at shows and allows the judges to examine the cats and discuss their proposed standard. These breeds may be registered and shown in miscellaneous but are not yet accepted for provisional status and can receive no awards.

Household Pet competition is for all non-pedigreed cats. Entries cannot be missing any of their extremities. Kittens must be between four and eight months of age on the first day of the show, and all cats older than eight months of age must be neutered or spayed.

AWARDS AND PRIZES

Registered unaltered cats are eligible to compete for champion and grand champion titles. All cats begin in the open class, where they compete against other cats of the same breed, sex, and color for first (a blue ribbon), second (a red ribbon), and third (a yellow ribbon). The first-place winner also receives a red, white, and blue winners' ribbon. A cat becomes a champion when he or she has six winners' ribbons. Champions are eligible to compete against other champions for points to become a grand champion.

After the judge has finished judging the cats in the open class by breed, division, and color, he or she begins with the champions. The male and female champions are each given first, second, and third place ribbons. Then the judge repeats the process with the grand champions.

Only after all the cats in a color group have been judged will the judge give the best of color class (a black ribbon) and second-best of color class (a white ribbon) to the winners. After the colors and breeds or divisions have been judged, the judge will award the best of breed/division (a brown ribbon), second-best of breed/division (an orange ribbon), and finally the best champion of breed/division (a purple ribbon). The best champion of breed receives one point for each

There are six categories in a CFA show. The kitten on the right would be judged in the Kitten competition, while the cat on the left would be judged in the Championship competition.

champion he or she defeated. These points are added up until the cat achieves 200 points, at which point he or she becomes a grand champion.

Spayed and neutered cats (premiers) are judged the same way. Six winners' ribbons are needed to become a premier, but the cat only needs 75 points to become a grand premier, because not as many altered cats are shown.

The finals occur after a judge has examined all the cats in either the all-breed competition or specialty show. The judge presents his or her picks for the top ten cats in show. Remember, each ring is a separate show.

Most cat shows provide the judges with plastic ribbons that can be reused and wiped off. You are invited to collect a fabric ribbon equal to what your cat has won from the judges' table. Many exhibitors only collect the colorful rosettes awarded for the best in show, and some will have the judge autograph the ribbon or rosette as a memento.

You can go home after cleaning your benching area to bask in your cat's glory and plan for the next show.

CAT REGISTRY ASSOCIATIONS

American Association of Cat Enthusiasts
P.O. Box 213
Pine Brook, NJ 07058
Phone: 973-335-6717
Fax: 973-334-5834
E-mail: info@aaceinc.org
Web: *www.aaceinc.org/welcome.html*

American Cat Fanciers Association
P.O. Box 203
Point Lookout, MO 65726
Phone: (417) 334-5430
Fax: (417) 334-5540
E-mail: info@acfacat.com
Web: *acfacat.com*

Australian Cat Federation (Inc)
Post Office Box 3305
Port Adelaide SA 5015
Phone: 08 8449 5880
Fax: 08 8242 2767
E-mail: acf@catlover.com
Web: *www.acf.asn.au*

Canadian Cat Association
220 Advance Blvd,
Suite 101
Brampton, Ontario
Canada L6T 4J5
Phone: (905) 459-1481
Fax: (905) 459-4023
E-mail: office@cca-afc.com
Web: *www.cca-afc.com*

The Cat Fanciers' Association, Inc.
P.O. Box 1005
Manasquan, NJ 08736-0805
Phone: (732) 528-9797
Fax: (732) 528-7391
E-mail: cfa@cfainc.org
Web: *www.cfainc.org*

Cat Fanciers Federation
P.O. Box 661
Gratis, OH 45330
Phone: 937-787-9009
Fax: 937-787-4290
E-mail: cff@siscom.net
Web: *www.cffinc.org*

Cat Federation of Southern Africa
P.O. Box 25
Bromhof 2125
Rep. of South Africa
Phone or Fax: +27 11 867-4318
E-mail: webmaster@cfsa.co.za
Web: *www.cfsa.co.za*

Federation Internationale Feline
Ms. Penelope Bydlinski
Little Dene
Lenham Heath
Maidstone, Kent
GB-ME17 2BS
Phone: +44 1622 850913
Fax: +44 1622 850908
E-mail: penbyd@compuserve.com
Web: *www.fife.org*

Federazione Italiana Associazioni Feline
c/o Rag. Cesare Ghisi
Via Carlo Poma n.20
46100—Mantova
Phone: 0376-224600
Fax: 0376-224041
E-mail: fiafmn@mynet.it
Web: *www.zero.it/fiaf*

The Feline Control Council of Victoria, Inc.
Royal Melbourne Showgrounds
Epsom Road
Ascot Vale,
Victoria 3032, Australia
Phone: (03) 9281 7404
Fax: (03) 9376 2973
E-mail: m.jones@rasv.metbourne.net
Web: *www.hotkey.net.au/~fccvic*

Governing Council of the Cat Fancy
4-6 Penel Orlieu
Bridgwater, Somerset,
TA6 3PG. (UK)
Phone: +44 (0) 1278 427 575
E-mail: GCCF_CATS@compuserve.com
Web: *ourworld.compuserve.com/homepages/GCCF_CATS/welcome.htm#office*

International Cat Exhibitors, Inc.
P.O. Box 772424
Coral Springs, FL 33077-2424
Web: *members.aol.com/jhagercat/ICE.htm*

The International Cat Association, Inc.
P.O. Box 2684
Harlingen, TX 78551
Phone: 956-428-8047
Fax: 956-428-8047
E-mail: ticaeoe@xanadu2.net
Web: *http://www.tica.org*

United Feline Organization
218 NW 180th Street
Newberry, FL 32669
Phone and fax: 352-472-3253
Email: UFO1FL@worldnet.att.net
Web: *www.aracnet.com/~ltdltd/ufo.htm*

World Cat Federation
Hubertstraße 280
D-45307 Essen, Germany
Phone: +49 201/555724
Fax: +49 201/509040
E-mail: wcf@nrw-online.de
Web: *home.nrw-online.de/wcf/english/ehome.html*

INDEX